SCOTLAND
the brief

A SHORT HISTORY OF A NATION

CHRISTOPHER HARVIE

cheerfully illustrated
by Scoular Anderson

ARGYLL✤PUBLISHING

© Christopher Harvie
2010

Argyll Publishing
Glendaruel
Argyll PA22 3AE
Scotland
www.argyllpublishing.com

The author has asserted
his moral rights.

**British Library
Cataloguing-in-
Publication Data.
A catalogue record for
this book is available
from the British
Library.**

ISBN 978 1 906134 61 7

Printed in the UK by
J F Print Ltd.,
Sparkford, Somerset

in memory of
Angus Calder,
historian, and
John Burnie,
engineer

Contents

Preface

I HAVE tried to write an account of Scotland which conveys the basic historical facts. It stemmed from my realisation, touring schools as a Member of the Scottish Parliament and showing visitors around, that not enough had been done to make either group aware of the narrative of the country's history. So it's meant to be read by those of all ages coming to it for the first time.

Scottish history suffers from Anglocentrism – you could call it 'metromania' – to the degree that you can't extract a believable Scotland from most 'British' histories. And you therefore can't relate the country to great historical, economic and cultural movements which swept over the world – many of which it influenced. I have tried to give a robust account, with an easily-accessible 'bookstore', and a guide to accessible sources, illustrative material and historical sites. A summing-up traces the interweaving of what Edwin Muir called 'the story and the fable' and shows how, in history-teaching, we can match the local to the global.

The book shares the sources and therefore the debts to colleagues and friends who helped in my *Short History of Scotland,* Oxford, 2002 (you know who you are) but is a reinterpretation with young people and visitors in mind. So it was rethought and written in trains and buses and bed-and-breakfasts, and owes much to the ingenuity of Derek Rodger: not least the contribution of Scoular Anderson. Profits from it will go to the Scottish Association for Public Transport, which celebrates its fiftieth anniversary in 2011.

Christopher Harvie
Melrose, 15th August 2010

PART 1
THE COMMUNITY
OF THE REALM

The Romans invaded Scotland in 43AD
– did it rain all the time?

1. Ice-sheet to Caledonia

BC 10,000 to AD 500

IN THE 1780s there was a great debate over the origins of the earth. Did it evolve from a fireball or a mudball? The first group, the Vulcanists, was headed by a Scotsman, James Hutton, the second, the Neptunians, by the German Abram Werner. The prize went to the Vulcanists, and the earth was seen as beginning in a fiery mass which, over thousands of millions of years, cooled, acquired moisture and ultimately sustained life.

Later ice ages cut into the ravaged coast of the west, eroded sands from volcanic rock, whose deposits were compressed and eroded again. Glaciers gouged valleys, and crushed the rotted remains of plants and trees, shells and early animals into limestone and coal.

Men turned up in what was then the British peninsula about 30,000 years ago, crossing a landbridge from Europe in the intervals of ice ages in which the land froze under hundreds of feet of ice, thawed for a time, then froze again.

Human beings in Scotland date back to about 10,000 BC, when hunter-gatherers moved north in search of animals for food and furs, and built small, seasonal settlements. Then they gradually herded and fished rather than hunted, and built more permanent wood and stone dwellings. They cleared much of the forest that extended over the land after the ice retreated and their politics seem to have been of rather aristocratic or priestly grandeur, with ritual sites and temples of great leaders, such as the Callanish stone circle on Lewis and the tomb of Maes Howe on Orkney

Though checked by lack of transport and information about sophisticated technology, these people were no less intelligent than we are today. The Skara Brae settlement on Orkney (3100 BC) shows the locals making use of stone panels as ingenious as anything in an Ikea flat-pack, constructing shelves, stores, fishponds, lockable doors. Callanish or Maes Howe suggest sophisticated elites creating works which enabled them to keep the seasons for fishing and stock-breeding.

Moving on from herding beasts to tilling the soil, this grandeur later seems to have given way to independent farms and villages, while in the bronze and iron ages (which made weapon-making easier) defensive fortresses and enclosed fields developed.

Again, our images are filtered through national myths and the ingenious arguments of the 1700s. The writer and economist Adam Smith in *The Wealth of Nations*, placed the origins of international trade in the eastern Mediterranean. The reality was a westward migration of the Celtic tribes of Hallstatt and La Tene (named after great hoards in Austria and Switzerland) about 800-500 BC. Only during the period of Greek dominance (500-100 BC) did recorders from outside come, with the geographer Ptolemy of Alexandria's map of 150 BC. This map was plotted by circumnavigating the archipelago that the Romans, its first *known* European conquerors, would call Britannia. Caledonia was its forbidding north.

The Roman invasions from 43 AD pushed deep into Scotland and then stabilised themselves on the fortified wall of Hadrian built in 121 AD between the Rivers Tyne and Solway. Northward of this were the *Foederati*, the 'Treaty people', a mix of Celtic tribes: Welsh (Pretani) in the south-west, Irish (Scoti) in the west, and north of the River Forth the Picti, the least accessible by sea and consequently the most mysterious.

As early as this, some enduring qualities of the place and its people were being made clear. Scotland was easy to invade, as long as sea-power was secured. The west coast was a better bet than the east; it had plenty of landmarks and sheltered waters. But there the easy part ended, particularly for a great land power like Rome. The sea was unreliable, but low-lying land was often impassable because of undergrowth and marshes.

To the Romans some of the locals were friendly and biddable farmers, up for villas and wine and a quiet life near roads, forts and ports; but others were herdsmen and fishermen, given a chance rustlers and pirates, and a pest. The goodwill of the first wasn't worth the burden of dealing with the second. For nearly three hundred years 'the last of the free' were contained, subjected to periodic invasions and one longish occupation as far as the Forth-Clyde Antonine Wall (142-185 AD), but largely left alone.

The Roman Empire was essentially land-based, founded on roads, camps and a well-organised army. In 314-24 AD it was supposedly made Christian by the Emperor Constantine, who also shifted its centre to Constantinople (now Istanbul), but it was increasingly subject to the movements of peoples. Not so

> Scotland may be small, but its people's interest in geography, trade and travel has marked the globe, both directly and through the maps and atlases turned out by Scots firms: Bartholomew, Johnston, Philips. The Ordnance Survey started here, after 1745.

much a surge of invasion than a Rome whose identity was diluted by other subject groups doing deals with more mobile groups from the east. This forced Saxon peoples westwards.

In Britannia they found suspicion but also a welcome and were in places incorporated into the Roman system and army. The latter, however, grew more and more troublesome as central control deteriorated. Revolts brought minor officers to power, the gentry in their villas tired of the upstarts, and the departure of the legions from Britannia in 410 AD was therefore not seen at the time as a disaster, until the whole centralised system fell apart.

'From the fury of the Northmen, Lord God deliver us!'

2. A Kingdom of Five Peoples

500–1066

WHAT FOLLOWED in the small Scottish lordships, paradoxically, wasn't the so-called Dark Ages but an astonishing creative output, which reached its climax in the seventh century in the illuminated books of Kells and Durrow, and the 'speaking' crosses of Celtic/Pictish Christianity. In the fifth century the Romano-Christian order was pressed by the Saxons to the islands and mountains of the west, in the period of St Ninian and St Patrick and St Mungo (mythic figures based on the activity of real priests, travelling between now-isolated Christian communities). Then, using the sea and rivers, the Celtic church undertook energetic missionary activity which covered – and converted – much of western Europe.

This was a distinctive social order: its members ranged from scholarly or contemplative monks to churchmen-diplomats politically engaged among the clans and small kingdoms. The Irish warrior-chief

---

Population: perhaps 200,000 under the Romans, rising to 0.6million by the time of the Black Death, 1350, then falling to 0.5m in 1500. In 1755 1.25m, 1801

Columba of the Ui Neil (521-97) turned holy man and established his monastic enclosure on the island of Iona in Dal Riata, later bringing the Pictish kingdom to the east, centred on Inverness, into the Christian sway.

Columba's biographer Adamnan publicised pilgrim travel to the Holy Land and established a principle of consideration for civilians in time of war: a first step in international law. This success, based on the sea-lanes and the wood-framed, skin-clad galley (rather like the Irish 'curragh') ended with the creation under the family of Kenneth McAlpin of a unified kingdom of the Picts and Scots, around 850, responding first to Northumbrian and later to Viking invasions, which began at the end of the eighth century.

The Northmen – Vikings was a later term – in their 'hydrodynamic' longships, swift under sail or oar, wooden clinker planking secured by iron nails, worked as great a revolution in Europe as Moslem cavalry did at the same time with their thoroughbred horses. Their initial raids were brutal thievery – 'From the fury of the Northmen, Lord God deliver us!' – but were soon followed by trade and religious conversion, and a powerful elite rule ranging from northern France to Sicily and Russia. They settled (first official census) 1.6m, in 1901 4.6m and in 2001 5.1m. Emigration has cut most of the natural increase. Sweden, 4.5m in 1901, went to 9m in 2010.

in Orkney and Shetland and along the western seaboard, which became a junction for further colonies in the Faroes, Iceland, Greenland and briefly 'Vinland' in North America. Their sagas, notably the *Heimskringla* (c.1230) showed a complex proto-democratic politics (the first parliament was at Thingveillir in Iceland in 930) and their influence on Scotland great, although Orkney and Shetland didn't become Scots until 1472.

The outcome of this period was remarkable: the creation of a political structure that stretched across five ethnic groups – Scots, Picts, Britons, Inglis and Norse, and held them in some sort of unity. This was unique in early medieval Europe, and its imperial pretension was apparent in the names – David (Israel), Constantine (Rome), Alexander (Greece), Robert (Sicily) – the Scots kings gave themselves. The way they were elected was less inspirational – the general practice was a short sharp war which established the best-qualified.

The last of these Celtic kings was Macbeth, 1040-57, by all accounts a reasonable ruler (first to visit Rome) traduced by Shakespeare, but overthrown in turn by Malcolm, married to a princess of the Saxon royal line, who fell, raiding into England, in 1093.

Out of the feuding of Norman (and Scots) families
comes a nation

3. Living with
Norman England

1066–1320

WITH KING MALCOLM and Margaret – she was later made a saint and her tomb at Dunfermline became a great place of pilgrimage – and their son David I, Scotland moved towards a more centralised, religiously-sanctified monarchy, with a southern border running along the ridge of the Cheviot Hills. But it was still one distanced from the pattern prevailing in England, in which the Norman Duke William rapidly pushed out the Saxon nobility after the Battle of Hastings in 1066.

The gradual immigration of Anglo-Norman nobility or merchants from France, Brittany and Flanders (many of whom also held land in England, and were vassals to the English king) was partly countered by the Scots kings' careful cultivation of the church through building monasteries. This was at a time when the power of the Pope was growing, expressed

in the First Crusade (1096-99) and steadily develop-
ing in the twelfth century. In 1175, a particularly weak
moment for the Plantagenets, Norman rulers of
England, the Scots persuaded the Pope to recognise
the Archbishopric of Glasgow as a 'special daughter':
directly under Rome instead of under the English
Archbishop of York. They would make much use of
this in future.

At this date more than half of the population spoke
Gaelic, with Inglis confined to the south-eastern part
and the more northerly coasts with which it commun-
icated. Berwick, on the English border was the largest
town, one of those given the status of burghs by King
David, chiefly as a means of raising royal revenue
from an establishment of immigrant merchants.

The twelfth and thirteenth centuries were a period
of peaceful coexistence between the two countries,
although the Scots found themselves being embroiled
in the unstable politics of the south. The latter part
of the thirteenth century, however, saw a new
purposiveness in English policy, with the career of
Edward I.

Edward had crusaded, and had stabilised his
Norman inheritance in Gascony (South-Western
France). In the 1280s he conquered the Welsh. He

> 'If a man were permitted to make all the ballads,
> he need not care who should make the laws of a
> nation'
> Andrew Fletcher of Saltoun, 1704

was an archetype of modernising, integrative nationalism and he did not intend to stop at Wales when he was given his chance by the accidental death of Alexander III in 1385. Alexander's heiress was the daughter of the Norwegian king, but she died on the sea crossing. He was then asked to arbitrate between the various claimants to the Scots throne, and in 1292 chose the most pliable, John Baliol. But after humiliations from Edward, Balliol treated for alliances with France and Norway. The French alliance, later denoted the 'Auld Alliance' of 1295, would last until the Reformation of 1560.

The kingdom of France had lately expanded from a parcel of land around Paris, but was still threatened by family rifts and the English in Gascony. It was not able to do much to help the Scots. Edward invaded, sacked Berwick and occupied the lowlands. The nobles were divided, many fancying their own families' chances under him. His problem was that war was all right when it paid for itself, but once an army had to be kept in the north, the exchequer was under pressure both from parliament and from shipowners and contractors. Probably for this reason, Edward was particularly ruthless, seeking a rapid knockout before he ran into more trouble with France.

The Scots mobilised a 'national army' under Sir Andrew de Moray and William Wallace, and in 1297 inflicted a severe defeat on Edward's army at Stirling Bridge, the key junction-point between the Lowlands and Highlands. Moray represented the north, Wallace Lanarkshire: they indicated that the struggle was not a family one, but something like a national resistance. Wallace was later given the style of 'Guardian of Scotland', a national hero while de Moray, who died of wounds, was forgotten.

Two further invasions took place, Edward throwing in troops from Gascony and Wales. His longbowmen defeated Wallace's 'schiltrons' (packed masses of spearmen) at Falkirk. Wallace was subsequently hunted down, betrayed in 1305, and brutally executed in London. Robert Bruce, Earl of Carrick, then proclaimed himself king. Edward retaliated against Bruce's kinsmen. What had started as a family feud became, through Bruce's tactical skills and Highland alliances, a conflict raging throughout the country.

Edward organised a final invasion in 1309, but died at Burgh-by-Sands, near Carlisle. His son Edward II, first Prince of Wales, called it off, but returned in 1314 to relieve his garrison at Stirling Castle. Bruce had by then either defeated or converted his rivals in the north and Hebrides, and just south of the fortress, at Bannockburn, defeated a larger Edwardian force by making skilful use of terrain and traitors in the enemy ranks.

The War of Independence would go on and only be 'won' after Bruce's death in 1328, but it produced in 1320 a literary monument which would set the tone of the country's politics far beyond its time and place. The letter of the Scots nobles, clergy and 'community of the realm' to Pope John XXII, called the Declaration of Arbroath, endorsed King Robert, but ended with the ringing words:

> For we fight not for honour or glory but for freedom, which no good man gives up but with his life.

Its ideas came from the supporters of Thomas a Becket against King Henry II, and the stirring passage may be from Dante's *Purgatorio*, but it seemed to symbolise a new and more democratic idea of nation and liberty. The new Pope ignored it, but it was translated into Scots and incorporated into his epic *The Brus* by Archdeacon Barbour in 1375. Such poetry would become central to the Scots' heritage.

'Salmon, hides, wool out, silks and books in.'
Terms of trade are fun for the Scots nobility.

4. Auld Alliance and New Learning

1328–1541

IN 1359-60 vast impersonal forces struck again when the bubonic plague swept across Europe, cutting populations down by between a third and a half. Scotland seems to have got off fairly lightly, because its people were thinly distributed. There were then about a million and a half of them: perhaps a quarter died. This may have meant that an older social order persisted longer than elsewhere in Europe, where the 'Black Death' led to economic change and the early development of 'proto-industrialisation' – a capitalism based on agricultural settlements and domestic industrial production.

In Scotland the alliance with France, which plague hit as badly as England, would continue until 1560. It did little for trade, which stagnated, while the pound Scots fell. The only times that French troops were stationed in Scotland, in the late fourteenth and mid-sixteenth centuries, they were resented almost as much as the English, in the latter case even more.

But the alliance gave chances to the ambitious and educated: as mercenaries and scholars and lawyers in the service of the French king. It was from the Universities of Paris and the 'French' Popes at Avignon that careers were possible which were unthinkable in Scotland, and in due course these bred innovations in Scotland in the Universities of St Andrews (1411), Glasgow (1451) and Aberdeen (1495). In 1485 the Scots Church was finally given metropolitan status, although in fact this opened it to the predatory activities of the royal family and the greater nobles. 'Bonds of manrent' – somewhere between insurance covenant and oath – provided security to the middling folk in a society where 'kin', 'clan' and 'family' counted a great deal.

The style of the French came north, in the fashions and food of the court – particularly a taste for Bordeaux wine, the sophisticated design of Scots buildings, such as the royal palaces of Linlithgow, Falkland and Holyrood, and an awareness of European intellectual advance. In the fifteenth and sixteenth centuries, when England was a cultural desert because of persistent and degrading civil war,

Scottish literature and poetry in particular – personified by King James I, William Dunbar, Robert Henryson, Bishop Gavin Douglas – was among the most advanced in Europe in terms of content, language and rhyme-scheme.

This did little for the ordinary Scots folk, still – over 80% of them – living on the land in townships of 12-15 families, cultivating their strip-fields with cumbersome ox-ploughs. But it seems the Scots thrived on diets which included a lot of meat and fish: not something that would last.

Trade had been restricted by the hostile country that now lay between Scotland and Europe, but urban life now started to develop an economic culture of its own, based on exporting wool, salted salmon and animal skins (the basis of leather), and importing metal and luxury goods. Edinburgh in particular rose as the royal family settled on it as their most favoured capital. In the Low Countries the Scottish staple (a trading centre of Scots citizens observing Scots Law) moved in 1540 from Bruges to Dutch Veere, in Zealand, where it would stay until 1799.

The Stewarts – the name suggests their origin as court officials (stewards) – succeeded the ailing grandson of the Bruce in 1406. The five successive Jameses proved an intelligent dynasty, and through hard-fought military campaigns gradually freed themselves from over-mighty nobles like the Douglases or the MacDonald Lords of the Isles who ruled large tracts of the country as if they were personal property.

But overall their pretensions frequently ended in disaster. How grand they were can still be seen in the complex spires of St Giles, Edinburgh and Linlithgow Kirks, and the University of Aberdeen: imperial crowns which underlined the dynasty's intention of cutting a dash in Europe.

This was easier than taking on the English directly: the north of England was far poorer than the Scottish borders, and most Scottish invasions ended in defeat, often catastrophic, and bruising counterattacks. Once England withdrew from France, in 1453, and turned to sorting out the politics of the British Isles, Scotland would be under sustained threat.

This coincided with zenith of the Stewarts under James IV (1488-1513), intelligent and progressive, cultivated and arrogant: the would-be founder of a Scottish navy. He was initially diplomatic enough to

---

Stewart or Stuart? The first was original, Stewart
meaning 'steward' in Scots.
The French hadn't a 'w' so Mary of Guise and her
daughter rejigged the name to Stuart.

---

get power over the Church into his own hands, and
to conclude a treaty of perpetual peace with King
Henry VII of England, new, Welsh and uneasy. In 1502
James married Henry's daughter Margaret in the
'Union of Hearts'. The court historian John Maier
wrote a wish-fulfilling *History of Great Britain*. But
a revival of Anglo-French hostilities after the
accession of Henry VIII led to a rash royal raid into
Northumberland in 1513 which ended in disaster
on Flodden Field.

Technology again favoured the English: artillery
and musketry cut down James and his Scots nobility.
As with Edward I, a defeat led again to a systematic
attempt to entrench English advantage which
rebounded on itself. The Scots people resisted and
forced the English back – from this time dates the
enduring local patriotism of the Border 'Common
Ridings' at Hawick and Selkirk – but James V's
attempt at a further invasion ended in disaster at
Solway Moss in 1541. He died only a few days later,
leaving Mary of Guise, well-connected in France, and
a baby daughter, Mary.

'Wrong but romantic.' Schiller, Verdi and Hollywood get
Mary Stuart into the movies

5. Rough Wooing and Reformation

1541-1603

THE TUDORS had modernised their state and were now a formidable international force. In 1536 Henry VIII split from the church of Rome for dynastic reasons: a Spanish bride who could not give him a male heir. The Pope would not allow an annulment of his marriage.

In 1542, with a son by Ann Boleyn, he tried to renew the union project. Not famous for tact, he chose a scorched earth policy and effectively drove the Scots into the arms of the French. The widow of James V, Mary of Guise, became Queen Regent and the infant Queen of Scots was sent to France and betrothed to Dauphin Francis.

But France's influence meant ironically that Scots supped with the ideologues of the reformed faith at the French universities. The Scots Reformation, when it came, would be the sophisticated urban Calvinism of Paris, Amsterdam and Geneva, not an attempt to repair a backward and corrupt domestic Catholicism after half a century of royal and noble pillage.

In fact there was little enough about ideas on either side: Mary of Guise and her daughter were clever, tactically flexible, and (compared with the Tudors) killed only a few protestants. Likewise, the grand Scottish nobles manoeuvred shrewdly. In 1560 the Earl of Hamilton (despite being Duke of Chatelherault) went over to the Lords of the Congregation, who had backed reformist preachers like John Knox and Andrew Melville. They thought France and Rome worse than the English, so they leagued with them at Berwick, February 1560, and ended the Auld Alliance by the Treaty of Edinburgh in July.

This was the country to which Mary Queen of Scots returned in 1561, as widow of the young French king. Athletic, healthy and amorous, she outmanoeuvred some reformers and married her cousin Henry Darnley in 1565. She bore a son but got caught up in court intrigue as Darnley became unstable (through syphilis?), and probably connived at a conspiracy to kill him in 1567 involving the protestant Earl of Bothwell, who became first her lover, then her husband.

A Reformation Parliament in August 1660

separated Scotland from Rome with the 'Confession of Faith', but the *First Book of Discipline*, a blueprint for a 'Godly Commonwealth' based on a federation of parishes, presbyteries, synods, with at the summit a General Assembly of the Kirk, remained declaratory. Reformers ran into conflict with the nobility, but the educational ambitions survived, producing in 1595 an Act anent Education which promised a school in every one of Scotland's 1800 parishes.

Jamie the Saxt approached all problems
with an open mouth, but lived

6. The Wisest Fool

1603-1625

MARY'S INFANT SON, James VI, was thrown about like a ball between feuding nobles, interfering English and French. He was beaten by his tutor George Buchanan, Europe's greatest classicist and a theoretical republican. But he was, through his grandmother Margaret, Elizabeth's legitimate heir, in an age where English (if not Scots) monarchic theory made much of this. Shakespeare would in Macbeth furnish him with divine right and a claim to the throne.

On 24th March 1603 Elizabeth died. The Scottish king quickly posted south, attended by numerous ambitious aristos, hangers-on and the handsome young men he liked to have around him. He would not return for fourteen years. 'For the king,' wrote an English courtier, 'every day will be Christmas.'

No-one much liked James, though his admiration for himself was sincere, and to some degree deserved. He was a survivor and reigned until 1625. He

James invented 'Great Britain' to try to stop Scots
and English brawling about precedence. Which
brings us to 'Scots', 'Scottish', 'Scotch' and

managed to dismantle the power of the great nobles,
and constrain that of the Kirk. He commissioned the
monumental translation of the Bible (which effectively
ended the career of Court Scots as a literary language)
and prided himself that the government of Scotland
ran smoothly while he signed the papers in London
(he fixed the Parliament by nominating its executive,
'the Lords of the Articles'). He had much more trouble
with the growing English Puritan force at Westminster, and those who had done well out of looting
Spain and disliked his conciliatory policy.

James thought European. He encouraged his
Danish wife Anne – a grand patron of English culture
at perhaps its zenith: Shakespeare, Donne, Jonson,
Inigo Jones, Dowland, Tallis, Milton – to revert to
Catholicism, in order to open a dialogue with Catholic
Europe. But his daughter Elizabeth was married to
Prince Frederick of Nassau and he had favoured his
claims on the Kingdom of Bohemia.

In 1618 this produced disaster. The Bohemians
insulted the Catholic Habsburg who was Holy Roman
Emperor. He destroyed them, and the minor German
rulers closed ranks and retaliated. For thirty years
Germany would be devastated by Protestant and
Catholic armies. Good times for Scottish

---

problems! The first two are broadly interchange-
able: Scots (of people: Scots Guards) Scottish (of
things: Scottish scenery). Scotch is archaic but *not*
English.

---

mercenaries, remitting money back to their wives
and children in their tower houses, still built for
defence in an age where battlements and stout doors
made for good neighbours.

This wasn't the only sort of enterprise on the go.
With limited woodland, the Scots had exploited coal
for centuries, and some Jacobean magnates, like the
Bruces of Culross, whose Palace is conserved by the
National Trust, were industrialists on a grand scale.
Scots fisheries supplied all of north Europe, Presbyt-
erians being quite in favour of supplying fish to
Catholic Friday diners, though the carrying trade was
in Dutch hands.

Edinburgh, its choc-a-bloc 'lands' and wynds
perched above the Lothian plain, was by far the
largest town, and a hotbed of Presbyterian enthusiasm, hosting the assembly and opening its
municipal, Calvinist university. Elsewhere Calvinism
was variable in impact, and there were substantial
rural areas where it made no impact at all.

'An' the king lost his heid, puir gentleman. Mebbe it wasna' a very guid heid, but he was sair in need o' it.'

7. Covenant and Commonwealth

1625-1660

JAMES, like Elizabeth, was a survivor and knew how to dodge and weave. His son Charles I was moral and cultivated but small in stature and intellect. In the 1630s he tried to rule without Parliament, to make the Anglican church the instrument of royal authority, and then to impose both on the Scots. The result triggered the English Civil War, more recently reinterpreted as 'The War of the Three Kingdoms'.

It started with the Scots clergy and nobility appealing to the Calvinist people in the National Covenant of 1638, signed publicly in the new Greyfriars kirkyard in Edinburgh. The King attacked but the Scots, aided by soldiers like Alexander Leslie with plenty of experience in the German wars, defeated his army and cut off coal supplies to London by taking Newcastle. The Irish took advantage of this to revolt and in London Charles had to recall parliament. He intrigued clumsily, betrayed his supporters like Laud and Strafford, who were executed, then counter-attacked. War broke out.

The Scots mobilised again, this time in alliance with Parliament, in the Solemn League and Covenant of 1643, its aim being to impose Presbyterianism on the English. Initially this was successful, but then the brilliant tactics of the royalist Marquis of Montrose, commanding Highland and Irish troops, paralysed the Scots, while the first parliamentary offensives flopped in England. This led to the creation by Oliver Cromwell in 1645 of his New Model Army: a force upholding unprecedented efficiency over religious dogmatism.

Checked by this, the Scottish Presbyterians went back to the Stewarts: Charles promised what they demanded. But Cromwell's forces captured the king and in 1649 tried and executed him. The Scots continued to resist on behalf of his son, now Charles II, so Cromwell invaded and almost by chance devastated their main army at Dunbar. Charles himself landed at the mouth of the Spey in 1652, gathered the rest of the Scots army, marched to Worcester, and was thrashed there as well.

European scholars marvelled at the *praefervidium ingenium Scotorum* (amazing ingenuity of the Scots). James Mill wrote an eight-volume History of India (1818) without ever visiting.

Cromwell then consolidated his power in Scotland, abolished the parliament, and ruled the country directly – and remarkably fairly – by Major-Generals until he died in 1658.

Something remarkable happened in these hectic years. The English political philosopher Thomas Hobbes captured it in his political treatise *Leviathan*, which emphasised the fact that sovereign power, based in the last analysis on military force and not contract, governed social relations. So much for Presbyterian notions of 'federal Calvinism' or Covenants! In coming international confrontations *force majeure* and the English notion of 'Crown Imperial' would win out over the Scottish idea of the 'Godly Commonwealth', and circumstances would force many Scots to embrace this destiny.

Not least in still-Catholic Ireland where Stewart monarch and Protector alike found it advantageous to 'plant' former Protestant rebels, many from the Border districts (given to cattle thieving and family conflicts),to hold down the natives recently conquered in Ulster – storing up much trouble for later centuries.

Darien – right place, 200 years too soon

8. Glorious Revolution, Deadly Decade

1660-1698

CROMWELL'S RULE in Scotland was, like all attempts to control the place in detail, punitively expensive. The Commonwealth ended in 1660 when the General commanding, George Monck, lost patience with Cromwell's incompetent son Richard and marched on London. The man he restored, Charles II, intelligent, cultivated, serially promiscuous and thoroughly untrustworthy, knew Scotland enough to dislike it intensely. He restored the parliament but ordered it about through a trusted Governor, first the Earl of Lauderdale and then his own Catholic brother, James, Duke of York.

Like his grandfather, Charles was determined to bring bishops into the Kirk to supervise the Presbyterians, the unruliest of whom styled themselves the true Covenanters and smouldered in the south-west. Brutal guerrilla attacks and repression

To some in Scotland, William III is still the most
famous horseman ever, the centre of the Orange
Order whose ultra-Protestant parades every July
keep the seventeenth century alive. Historians point

ensued, recorded by Presbyterians like the Reverend
Robert Wodrow and the creators of monuments to
the martyrs, still to be found in lonely Galloway glens.

Attempts by the tactless Duke of York to impose
his own ideas on Edinburgh society also caused
rebellions by the lawyers and academics of the town,
and the emergence of a proto-nationalist in the shape
of the soldier and political philosopher Andrew
Fletcher of Saltoun, who joined (and practically
destroyed) the fruitless Monmouth rebellion against
James, now king, in 1685. Fletcher represented the
old Scots idea of an elective monarchy, but also the
notion of a decentralised, non-imperial Britain.
Circumstances were to force him into a minority.

The initiative to get rid of James came from
England, not from Scotland. The Whig nobility
appealed in 1688 to his brother-in-law Prince William
of Orange, *Statthalter* of the Netherlands, to displace
him, and William landed at Torbay in Devon. Too
incompetent to raise any sort of counterforce in
Scotland, James fled from London to France. A
Highland rising on his behalf petered out after its
leader James Claverhouse, scourge of the Covenanters and now Viscount Dundee, was killed at Killie-
krankie in 1689, and his campaign in Ireland ended

out that at the Battle of the Boyne, 1 July 1690,
Pope Alexander VIII supported William, but Scottish
sectarianism is beyond history.

with defeat at the Boyne, 1 July 1690. Kirk and
Parliament rejoiced in a specifically Scottish Glorious
Revolution and the return of their liberties after more
than a century of constriction, with the abolition of
the hated Bishops and of the Lords of the Articles.

Then things started to go horribly wrong. The
1690s was a 'little ice age' which devastated Scotland
and its European trading partners. Trade to the
north-east was drying up, and famine years in 1693-
8 in which thousands died, and poverty grew.

In an attempt to break out, a bold speculator
William Paterson, founder of the Bank of England in
1694, organised the Bank of Scotland and the
'Company of Scotland trading to the Indies' in 1695.
New Edinburgh would rise on the isthmus of Darien
in Central America, over which a new road would
link the Atlantic and Pacific. Two thousand colonists
were sent out, in two expeditions, but England and
Spain combined to isolate the Scots, the isthmus
proved a fever-pit and only about 300 eventually
returned, Paterson (remarkably enough) among
them, to a country financially ruined by the enterprise.

PART II
IMPERIAL PARTNER

Rogues, parcelling out a nation?
'Every man full of his own merit, and afraid of everyone
near him.' Daniel Defoe

9. Union

1698-1715

ALL THIS TIME, the might of France had been increasing, directed by Louis XIV and his ministers. But France, in its unified state, was about twice the size of Great Britain. At this time Ireland, its Catholics crushed after the campaigns of 1688-90, was fairly quiescent, but Scotland was not. There was the risk that it would resume an independent foreign policy, fuelled by the resentments generated by the Darien failure, and offer France a way in by the back door.

On the other hand, Darien left many like Paterson believing that formal parliamentary union with England was the best way out. It wasn't as if the Parliament offered all that much to the Scots. Its electorate was tiny, compared to that of England: a few score freeholders in each county, and town councils who nominated their own successors. Perhaps 4500 voters in all, out of a population of nearly two million.

There were alternatives. The Kirk had its General

Assembly, meeting every year for three weeks, in charge of poor relief and education, and general social discipline. The four universities were independent, and lawyers had their own governing body in the Faculty of Advocates. The towns had the Convention of Royal Burghs, which also controlled overseas economic policy. Parliament, under the Lords of the Articles, hadn't been allowed to interfere with any of these. Should it now be allowed to do so?

The people who did have a surfeit of autonomy were the nobles, who had thrived as the monarchy had declined. The Douglas Dukes of Hamilton, the Campbell Dukes of Argyll, possessed 'heritable jurisdictions', monarch-like privileges which could not be brought under the purview of London ministers. Since it was evident that Queen Anne, daughter of William and Mary, was unlikely to produce an heir, attention focused on the next-in-line, the Elector of Hanover, descended from James I's daughter Elizabeth, the Winter Queen of Bohemia.

So the Scottish MPs and more importantly the noblemen who sat with them in the parliament, had to be brought to London, by 'stuffing their mouths with gold', and ensuring that the Commissioners who were to negotiate the Treaty were pliable.

This itself wouldn't have been sufficient. What mattered to the non-noble elites, the burgesses and the lawyers and the Kirk, was that their positions would be guaranteed. It was obvious that they would have to be won over: by compensation for the Darien losses, by subsidies to the linen industry and to coastal fishing. Significantly, the economic clauses of the Treaty were passed by greater majorities than the other parts.

There was in fact little enthusiasm for the Treaty of Union on either the Scots or the English side. It was quickly betrayed as a fundamental law (as the Scots liked to think of it) when the Scottish Privy Council was abolished in 1711, followed by a Patronage Act in 1712 which subjected the Kirk to the control of the local 'heritors' or principal landowners. The Treaty was nearly revoked by the Westminster parliament after less than a decade.

What it did imply, however, were important alterations in London politics. It was a significant strengthening of the Commons, and whoever managed them, over the Lords and of Parliament over the Court, something which underlay the long rule of Sir Robert Walpole, Britain's first effective Prime Minister, and his Scottish henchman Alexander Campbell, Duke of Argyll.

Charles Edward Stewart: Say 'Throne of Britain';
don't say 'Tin of Shortbread'

10. A Cause Lost Forever

1715-1759

THE TREATY OF UNION accepted in Edinburgh on 17th January 1707 effectively made the 45 surviving Scottish MPs and 16 peers (elected by a pre-Union total of 170) into a commodity, to be purchased by the English rulers. In return Scottish elites were allowed a great deal of autonomy in their own domestic affairs, lubricated by plenty of patronage.

By the 1720s this was beginning to take effect as through a combination of legal and illegal enterprise, the ports and merchants of western Scotland established a powerful position in the tobacco and later sugar trades. The Duke of Argyll's power, however, remained a Highland factor, chiefly because London worried about the threat coming from that region. When Queen Anne died in 1715, and 'the wee, wee German lairdie' Elector George of Hanover succeeded, Mar started a rebellion in the north, which got as far as the inconclusive field of Sherrifmuir near Stirling, and then dispersed. In 1719 a Jacobite army sailed into the River Forth on French ships, but couldn't land. The government's General George Wade laid out a network of military roads, 1725-37, to inhibit another attack.

Then in 1745 the young son of the Pretender James VIII and III, Charles Edward Stewart, landed at Lochailort, rallied Catholic and Episcopalian clans, and marched on Edinburgh, ironically along Wade's roads. He defeated a Hanoverian force just outside the city and commandeered Holyrood Palace (though the Castle held out against him) then headed south. His Highlanders got to within 100 miles of London, reaching Derby, then turned back.

Had a French army attacked Dover, things might have been different, but the Highlanders wanted to return home for seed-time, and Charles' army threatened to melt away. He still managed to defeat another Hanoverian force at Falkirk before being pinned down and destroyed at Culloden on 16th April 1746. He made his escape through the Hebrides. Despite a rich reward offered by the government, no clansman betrayed him.

But the traditional military tenures of the clans were now suppressed and the chiefs with their legal privileges converted into orthodox landowners. This was an experiment considered so risky that the government had to secure its defences, with one of Europe's greatest fortresses built only a few miles from Culloden at Fort George, 1747-69. This was what 'civilisation' literally meant: the replacement of 'military tenures' by the rule of state power and civil law. In practical terms, this meant the canny management of Scotland after the 1760s by the Dundas family of Edinburgh lawyers

The 1745 rebellion was disastrous for the Jacobite cause, yet by incorporating the Highlanders in the British Army the London government provided itself with a powerful weapon with which to extend its imperial involvement. Almost certainly, as a sixth of her forces, they turned the Seven Years' War of 1753-9 in Britain's favour, in Canada and India. The cause that was lost was that of the people of the Highlands, ill-led by the old order, and exploited by the new.

'These are my mountains,/ And these are my glens'
The Countess of Sutherland improving the Highlands

11. Improvement

1745-1900

MORE SCOTS fought for George II at Culloden than fought for Prince Charlie, the Young Pretender. The country was already beginning to modernise and urbanise with great speed, and the rebellion was cited to intensify this change, by arguing that without it, disorder would reign. The result was dynamic but scarcely democratic, and carried in its wake a quite conscious propaganda manipulated by those who benefited by it.

The old system of communal farming by townships was suppressed in favour of 'muckle fermers' (large tenants paying high rents for mixed farms) using systems of rotation, horse-ploughs, steadings to house their work-force, high-skilled though ill-paid. About a tenth of Scottish villages were totally rebuilt so that underemployed labourers could spin and weave or fish as well as work on the land. Such settlements were rapidly connected up with turnpike roads, canals were driven from Forth to Clyde and down the Great Glen, and horse-drawn railways linked mines and quarries with waterways.

A doctrine of education, social mobility and free markets, which would be codified in Adam Smith's *Wealth of Nations* (1776) was coupled with extensive social engineering. Any energies that might have confounded this were diverted to extending the British Empire. The process would be recorded in the 1790s, parish by parish, in the *Statistical Account of Scotland* organised by the great Caithness landlord Sir John Sinclair, and the exercise was repeated in the 1840s: a thirty-odd volume documentation unique in Europe.

On the basis of the *Statistical Account* the novelist John Galt wrote two 'theoretical histories' in 1821-22, *Annals of the Parish* and *The Provost* which made the whole process seem inevitable. At the time it was known as 'improvement', though some were more conscious of this than others. But it was notable that its opponents themselves seemed to accept that they were marginal forces: secessionists vainly trying to withstand the impersonal forces of 'progress'.

Probably no other country in Europe saw a middle class rise more rapidly through a system that turned all social relationships into forms of realisable capital. Meanwhile a cultural superstructure was created that made this tolerable to those whose lives were changed – and in most cases not improved – by it.

Much later, in the 1880s, 'the industrial revolution' and in the 1890s Professor W R Scott's phrase 'the Scottish Enlightenment' were coined to describe this highly conscious episode of modernisation.

The first motor of industrial change was the linen industry, traditionally the product of local flax-growers and handloom weavers. Innovations in bleaching – from sour milk to sulphuric acid – were brought in, and a market created in the slave-worked plantations of the West Indies and American colonies. By the end of the century slave-picked cotton was being spun on a far-larger scale in water-powered mills, some of them huge, and built in the Scots lowlands. (The most famous was New Lanark, built by David Dale and passed to his son-in-law Robert Owen.) Investment in these and the infrastructure that sustained them came from squeezing wages in favour of middle-class capital for investment in labour-saving equipment, turnpike roads and canals. Scots engineers were outstanding examples of a revolution in technology, involving the use of iron parts such as wheels, rails and beams (stronger than wood and of course fireproof), bricks, and machine-cut stone.

The most famous of Scots inventions was the steam engine, or rather James Watt's perfecting of

When in the 'Great Tea Race' the clipper 'Taeping'
beat the 'Ariel' by 20 minutes sailing from Foochow
(near Hong Kong) to the Pool of London in 1866,
99 days to cover 16,000 miles, the first was owned,

the crude and huge 'atmospheric' mine-pump of
Thomas Newcomen into an efficient supplier of rotary
motion which could pump out mines, haul wagons
and lifts full of coal, or power textile machinery. Watt's
patent dated from 1769, and his engines were built
in Birmingham; hardly twenty of them were actually
in use in Scotland by 1800.

But shortly afterwards steam engines were applied
to water transport by William Symington, on his
'Charlotte Dundas' tugboat on the Forth and Clyde
Canal, and in 1812 Henry Bell's 'Comet' took to the
Clyde with fare-paying passengers.

Such improvements also helped open up the huge
Monklands coal- and iron-field, east of Glasgow, in
the 1820s. This delivered a very high-grade iron for
castings, just as the market boomed with the first
high-performance locomotive-worked railways.
Scotland's first, the Garnkirk and Glasgow, opened
in 1831, only a year after George and Robert
Stephenson's Liverpool and Manchester. Within
eighteen years trains ran by the east and west coast
routes to London, and as far north as Aberdeen.
Thomas Cook had started his famous cheap
excursions, conveying the English in great numbers
to the Highlands and Hebrides, and in 1851 lots of

---

the second skippered by Anstruther men. In 1884
Sir Sandford Fleming, another Fifer, engineer to the
Canadian Pacific, got international sanction to
divide the world into 24 time zones.

Scots of all social classes to the Crystal Palace in London's Hyde Park. For the Scottish pioneer of industrial history, Samuel Smiles, the endless carriages of specials crossing the Royal Border Bridge at Berwick were the great endorsement of the Union.

This was the prelude to an astonishing half-century in which the Clyde basin literally became the workshop of the world: its greatest single concentration of locomotive- and ship-building and general engineering, whose triumphs ran from the Forth Bridge and Vienna's Prater Wheel to Cunard's 'Aquitania' and 'Queen Mary'. These were essentially based on a fusion of scientific knowledge and engineering skills in the 1850s which revolutionised the marine steam engine, from a low-pressure monster to a high-pressure multi-cylinder power-pack, and brought the age of sail to an end by 1900.

In turn these brought businesses which mechanised former handcrafts and service industries, like Europe's biggest factory churning out Singer sewing machines at Clydebank, Nairn's linoleum factory at Kirkcaldy, the hardware of the book trade, from papermaking to binding, or the numerous distilleries which provided the quickest way out.

'I'd rather be the cause o' one,
than be the death of twenty.'
Robert Burns on morality

12. Ploughmen Poets: Cities of Intellect

1603-1832

THE *STATISTICAL ACCOUNTS* showed a country of high literacy: This would be reinforced in every small town by a library and later a newspaper, and many literary and historical clubs and societies. Edinburgh and Glasgow went further and became major centres of publishing.

Scotland was a land of poets in the late middle ages: enough for the Calvinists of 1560 to appeal to the ordinary folk with their *Gude and Godlie Ballads*: rapping for the reformation! Thereafter the Kirk's hostility to theatre and dance clamped down on this, and talent would mainly be found on the cavalier side: the 'Castalian Band' of poets around James VI and during the Civil War, the Marquess of Montrose and the extraordinary Sir Thomas Urquhart of Cromarty. On the other hand the Border Ballads with their mixture of violence, vamping until ready, and heartbreaking beauty.

But I hae dreamed a dreary dream
Ayont the isle o' Skye.
I saw a dead man win a fight
And knew that man was I.

Covenanters had legends of persecution and resistance which looked like a proto-Western, and John Bunyan's *Pilgrim's Progress* soon found itself on every cottar's shelf. Early in the eighteenth century Allan Ramsay, an Edinburgh printer, collected folk songs and wrote a Jacobite drama, *The Gentle Shepherd*, which villagers staged for over a century.

The next episode was remarkable. In 1761 a literary laird, James MacPherson, claimed to have detected old Gaelic manuscripts on an epic scale. *Ossian* was a phenomenon of the *Lord of the Rings* sort and, many argued, a complete fake. On the other hand it influenced a whole generation of early romantics, notably Goethe, Napoleon and (most influential in the long term) the German Johann Gottfried Herder, who made the fateful link between language, culture and nationality.

MacPherson died a rich man; so too did Henry Mackenzie, the author of the tear-jerking *Man of Feeling*. Both have long fallen from fashion, but the 'sympathy' they set out to conjure up was taken seriously, notably by Adam Smith, who had started off his career as a lecturer on literature.

Much more positive was to come. Robert Fergusson, a young Edinburgh lawyer, revived Dunbar's bawdy, affectionate treatment of the capital in the 1760s, and in 1786 came *Poems, chiefly in the Scottish Dialect* by an unknown young farmer, Robert Burns.

Burns was first a success, then a cult. Perhaps only now are the Scots coming to terms with his genius as a poet of the love and patriotism he knew, and the equality and democracy that he foresaw. The son of an unsuccessful small farmer, he was exceptionally well educated. His reading was that of an enlightened citizen – Adam Smith, David Hume and James Thomson – and his politics were radical, sympathising with the American and French revolutions:

'From scenes like these, old Scotia's grandeur
springs,
That makes her lov'd at home, rever'd
abroad
Princes and lords
are but the breath of kings,

An honest man's the noblest work of God.'

His enjoyment of love – idealistic and erotic – was unqualified.

> 'Yestreen when to the trembling string
> The dance gaed thro' the lighted ha'
> To thee my fancy took its wing,
> I sat, but neither heard nor saw:
> Tho' this was fair, and that was braw,
> And yon the toast of a' the town,
> I sigh'd, and said amang them a',
> Ye are na Mary Morison.'

As George Orwell noted, this is poetry that pierces the heart.

Burns met, at Professor Adam Ferguson's house in Edinburgh, a polite and knowledgeable boy with a limp. This was the young Walter Scott, born in Edinburgh to a lawyer's family but brought up in the Borders, with its strong oral culture and the recent memory of invasion by English and Jacobites. Scott's first reputation was as a narrative poet, then after 1814 as a novelist, on the strength of the impact of *Waverley*, the story of a young and ingenuous Englishman, caught up in the 1745 rebellion and torn between the two sides. 'The Author of *Waverley*' remained officially anonymous for another score of books. He was a Tory and had Jacobite emotions, but was otherwise an 'improving' businessman – gas company and railway director – brought down in 1826 by his speculations in publishing.

Two other talents were the Ettrick Shepherd James Hogg, illiterate until his teens, then the writer of brilliant parodies and satires, and the dark and disturbing *Confessions of a Justified Sinner* (1822) and John Galt, who transformed the dry facts of the *Statistical Accounts* into a witty panorama of a society moving from old agriculture to new industry – and the New World. Galt shows that what happened in Scotland was almost outdone by the way her literary men – and some women, too – projected the country worldwide. They underwrote the popular enlightenment of the nineteenth century – adult education, medical reform, civic universities, cheap publishing. Some Englishmen mocked; more took advantage of it and muscled in.

By the end of the nineteenth century nearly half the Scottish population lived in the four main cities of Glasgow (one million), Edinburgh (450,000), Aberdeen (200,000) and Dundee (200,000). About 75% lived in towns, while the country folk, whose

---

Patrick Geddes, 1856-1932, had the gift of thinking
brilliant thoughts just as a guilt-ridden millionaire

---

numbers grew steeply until the 1870s, fell with the
downturn in the agricultural economy after cheap
grain and meat could be imported.

Scientific intellect had been important for the
Scots. In the seventeenth century it led the ambitious
to careers in the army or to attend universities like
Dutch Leyden. Back home there were the Edinburgh
clubs and publishers and increasingly art dealers
such as the Foulis brothers of Glasgow, who created
a taste for the classical among the city's middle
classes. The *Encyclopaedia Britannica*, modelled on
that of Condorcet and Diderot in Paris, began in
Edinburgh in 1769.

The regional intellect in Aberdeen was influenced
by the agri-capitalism of Buchan and the dealings of
the herring fishery, the common sense philosophy of
Thomas Reid and plentiful bursaries which meant
'Buchan loons and queans' becoming teachers
throughout the country in the new Board Schools of
1871.

Dundee first rose with the coarse linen industry,
then with whaling. These fused in the astonishing
rise of the jute industry, which provided the
packaging for Britain's dominance as an international
trader, and led to vast fortunes.

happened by. He got money from Carnegie, was revered by Nehru, inspired Roosevelt's Tennessee Valley Authority.

But Glasgow was altogether different in scale. Why? It was already a major clerical and educational centre in the Middle Ages, sited at the lowest ford on the Clyde. In the late seventeenth century it rose on the Atlantic trade, establishing a deep-water harbour near Greenock which became Port Glasgow. It was from here, and from ports as far south as Whitehaven in Cumbria (with a lot of smuggling thrown in), that the city flourished on the tobacco trade. By 1776 the city was booming, with linen coming up. The Clyde was deepened, a canal from Clyde to Forth projected and partly built, and the centre planned on an American-style gridiron pattern.

Glasgow was well-placed to take advantage of the next boom, in cotton, which marked the 1780s, and made Clyde cotton second only to that of Lancashire. More, this triggered advances in engineering and finance. The blackband ironstone of the Monklands, first exploited in 1829, completed the takeoff. By 1851 Glasgow's population was 345,000, trebling again by 1911. The downside was that this was achieved at the expense of living standards. High immigration and employment accompanied tiny, congested and unsanitary housing.

'We war with rude nature, and come off always victorious,
and loaded with spoils.' Thomas Carlyle

13. Rule Britannia!

1745-1914

PATRONAGE was one of the main drivers of the Union. The soldiers from 'cleared' Highland glens fought at the bidding of a generation of younger sons 'on the make', who risked their lives as officers or 'clerks' of the great London chartered companies, and expected rewards to match. Their breakthrough came even earlier than the fighting men, and cemented the dominance of the Scots in expanding the Empire. They had talked an ambitious game. Now they could use their less-fortunate kinsfolk to make the gamble work.

In the eighteenth century there were two main contested areas with the French: North America and India. In the first the Scots built up the trapping and fur business of the Hudson's Bay Company, and then leagued with friendly Red Indian tribes to expel the French. The fall of Quebec in 1759 was critical, and was shortly followed by the expulsion of the French from most of their East Indian territories, to the advantage of the likes of James Mill and a succession

71

Global heroes: Thomas Telford, master engineer
was a shepherd's son from Westerkirk. His money
founded Langholm Library. Another 'muckle
touner' William Mickle translated the Portuguese

---

of Scots governors, industrialists, plantation-owners.
Most of the 'nabobs' who survived (a minority) came
back loaded. Gentle Jane Austen didn't care for
people called Crawford or Dalrymple.

The Scot overseas was initially unreassuring.
Darien wasn't unique. In 1722 John Law of Lauriston
nearly destroyed France with his Mississippi Scheme.

To Burns the Scots aristo went off to Europe:

> To make a tour an' tak a whirl,
> To learn *bon ton* an' see the worl'.
> There at Vienna, or Versailles,
> He rives his father's auld entails;
> Or by Madrid he takes the rout,
> To thrum guitars and fecht wi' nowt.

But he (or his tutors, like David Hume and Adam
Smith) came back with the classic taste that created
both Edinburgh's New Town, and the 'national'
painting of Allan Ramsay Junior, Henry Raeburn and
David Wilkie.

After 1759 expansion was rapid: a mixture of
military victory and trading deals, many on the windy
side of the law. The English elites tended to mirror
the hierarchies of London and the cathedral cities

discovery epic the *Lusiads*. Christopher Grieve was born in the Library and read every book. Neil Armstrong, first man on the moon, got the burgh's freedom in 1972.

---

they were used to; the Irish moved into the big towns, where they provided the labour to be managed by shrewd Scots like John Young, the Ayr-born creator of the port of Montreal. Scots could also be found on the land, where the botanic garden, adapting plants to new habitats, became a major instrument of imperial expansion. Dock engineering, speculative suburbs, later on railways like the Canadian Pacific and urban tramways: the Scots attended to, and lived from, the institutions of the new colonies.

From the mid-nineteenth century they gained further prestige from missionary activity, combined with education in India and African exploration prestigious enough in the hands of Dr David Livingstone to drown out discussion of the cash brought in by firewater (whisky loosened up natives for conquest) and the opium trade for which the British subjugated the Chinese in the 1840s.

By the 1908-12 depression emigration was no longer a wrench or a gamble but a career option. Two Harvie great-uncles, architect and engineer, slipped smoothly from Motherwell into the Vancouver middle class; there was a class at Edinburgh's Royal High specially run for the Shanghai Bank. Usually, they stayed.

'From the lone shieling, and the misty island,
Mountains divide us, and a waste of seas.
But still the blood is strong, the heart is highland,
And we in dreams behold the Hebrides'

14. Reform

'Those whom the law neglects will always be enemies to law, and will always be dangerous, more or less.'

THE WORDS were those of a great Liberal and historian, of Gaelic descent, T B Macaulay.

Britain's was a liberal empire, and much of its effectiveness came from the free movement of its elites among the institutions of state.

The 1832 Reform Act wasn't achieved without a struggle, particularly in English towns, where the Castle of Nottingham and the Palace of Bristol were laid low. Scotland was quieter, but her intellectuals, running the *Edinburgh Review*, had done much to expand the agitation. The English electorate doubled, the Scots (extended by creating new urban constituencies) went up from 5000 to 65,000.

Reform, however, did little for the mass of the people. How were they to cope with dispossession on the land, and the often enforced flight into the towns? Up to the 1840s this upheaval seemed almost apocalyptic, and even among the well-off there thrived millenarian or utopian ideals.

Robert Owen, the owner of the New Lanark Mills and social experimenter, promoted his 'new view of society' on every possible occasion. His schemes usually collapsed, but they trained a generation of working-class activists who would eventually gain a qualified utopia in the Co-op societies. Chartism was political rather than social; its leaders, organised on a British basis, argued for their 'six points': universal manhood suffrage, equal electoral districts, payment of members, secret ballots, no property qualifications, and annual parliaments. Chartists were well organised, generally moral-force and legalistic, and ineffective. If you wanted to be a democrat, then go to Canada, or by the 1850s Australia and New Zealand. By the mid-century there were also civic careers to be made in the churches, in medicine, and in education. Tasks that would in Europe have gone to national parliaments were shared between Westminster and increasingly powerful Scottish burghs whose powers expanded to cope with the challenges of poverty, disease and pollution. These tasks lay before a country

Scots shoppers are criticised for encouraging supermarkets, yet they pioneered mass-marketing in the nineteenth century with Sir Thomas Lipton's chain stores and the branches of the Co-ops, which could take as much as 30% of local commerce.

particularly famous for the quality of its medical education, spectacularly realised in projects like Glasgow's water supply, piped from Loch Katrine in 1859.

'Municipal progress' was also cultural, as Glasgow's Art Gallery testified. Her young painters, the 'Glasgow Boys' and 'Scots Colourists' were an exhilarating change from academic portraits and stags at bay, and their School of Art by Charles Rennie Mackintosh, opened 1899-1910, became one of Europe's most admired buildings.

In 1867 the vote was conceded to urban male householders, and the first sustained campaign began for woman suffrage. They could soon vote for and sit on local councils and school boards, and gain access to universities and teaching hospitals although their parliamentary vote came only in 1918. The present single-member constituencies date from the Third Reform Act of 1884, but 'one person one vote' came as late as 1948.

15. A House Divided

1832-85

THE GREAT PUBLIC debate in Victorian Scotland was not, however, about politics but about religion. The issue of control of the Kirk had throbbed away, parish by parish, in the eighteenth century. But as political reform gained momentum, the religious issue moved alongside it. It had little to do with theology, much more with the Church's prominent social position – far greater than in any other European country – dominating education, poor relief, and social discipline.

To begin with, religious politics had consisted of 'seceding': stalking out of the Kirk while usually still claiming to embody it. But as the evangelical revival gained support, in the late eighteenth century and with the support of the Dundas family, the struggle returned to the parish. Shortly after the 1832 Act the evangelical party increased and, under its eloquent leader the Revd. Thomas Chalmers, became ever more influential. Not least because of its links

The Disruption drama was recorded by the artist
D. O. Hill and photographer Robert Adamson,
making up a huge crowd scene 'The Signing of the

with the press, which was expertly led by Cromarty stonemason and thinker, Hugh Miller, editor of *The Witness*.

After 1834 matters came to a head, as congregations resisted the 'intrusion' of lairds' nominees; actions were fought all through the Church courts and then, on appeal, to the Court of Session. Westminster Whigs didn't really want to know about the issue, since the Scots were unlike English non-conformists in wanting to retain an established church. The Tories wouldn't move against their aristocratic allies.

In 1842 the Home Secretary Sir James Graham threw the Kirk's 'Claim of Right' out. This provoked a walk-out of the leading evangelicals at the next General Assembly the following May to found the Free Church. Known forever after as the Disruption.

The Disruption brought no revival but an obsessive competition to build as many churches as possible. By the 1860s Scotland was over-churched, with up to six big half-empty gothic barns in every small town, but the actual conflict would limp on until Kirk reunion finally came in 1929.

It was probably in this decade that 'North Britain'

Deeds of Demission' from hundreds of individual calotypes. These were superb, the picture almost comic.

came closest to describing the place. But even then protests at governmental delays were starting to mount, and the creation of the Scotch Education Department in London in 1872 intensified the call for a Scottish Minister. Fear of the country following Ireland into agrarian revolt forced this concession – the revival of the Scottish Office under a Scottish Secretary – in 1885.

W. E. Gladstone led the Liberals to offer the Irish home rule a year later. This took until 1921 to gain, with much violence after 1916, when co-leader of the Dublin Rising was James Connolly from Edinburgh. But Gladstone's bill inspired Scots moves in favour of devolution. This mattered as much to Keir Hardie's Scottish Labour Party of 1888 as his socialist objectives.

16. Industry and Empire

1800-1914

'A UNION FOR EMPIRE' certainly provided lots of patronage, but this wasn't wholly welcome to Scots 'improvers'. Why? Adam Smith, for one, disapproved of the idea, which he called 'mercantilism', of building up national strength at the expense of other nations – though this described pretty fairly the relations between the states of eighteenth-century Europe.

The fringes of sharp trading practice – smuggling, piracy, downright fraud – were murky, and until late in the eighteenth century colonies were seen as captive markets, rather than as the source of raw materials: something that partly led to the American revolt in 1776.

This was a setback to Scotland the trading nation. The tobacco lords were badly hit. But trade bounced back in the shape of sugar and cotton, provided by the last phase of human slavery in the West Indies and America. Scots were not directly involved in the

'. . . and, all unseen, romance brought up the 9.15'
Rudyard Kipling

Golf probably came to Scotland from Holland; it reached London in 1603 with James VI and Calcutta in 1829, before provincial England (1860s) let alone America (1884). The Royal and Ancient Club codified the rules in St Andrews in 1853.

Africa-to-Caribbean slave trade, centred in Bristol and then Liverpool, but profited much from supplying the plantations with equipment, and building machinery to refine their products – spinning-frames, sugar boilers and so on.

This wasn't yet the world of steam-powered technology, but it gave birth to it. Think, for instance, of the Stevenson family, who built the intricate stone tower lighthouses of the Northern Lights which tamed the fierce coasts of the Hebrides and the Pentland Firth. Or of Telford, who saw his projects as 'a great working academy' and schooled such 'national technologists' as William Dargan in Ireland, John Ericsson in Sweden and the USA and Joseph Mitchell who built the Highland Railway.

After 1880 there was a scramble for territories between the European states. Had Scotland still been independent she might have picked up a few thousand square miles of jungle or desert somewhere. Empire, and the disinclination of English grandees to have much to do with trade in it, gave the Scots plenty of scope in places like Montreal, Singapore, and Hong Kong.

The Scots managed to stay on both sides of the argument, imposing British rule and exploitation, but often organising the resistance of settlers, or even natives, against it.

William Lyon MacKenzie headed the campaign for responsible government in 1830s Canada, Allan Hume founded the Indian Congress in 1885, Andrew Fisher was the first Labour Prime Minister of a federal Australia in 1908. By 2000 it was reckoned that 25 million Scots lived worldwide, small in comparison with a global population of 6.6 billion, but exercising disproportionate influence.

Though could an imperial race base itself on a working-class living in the tiny tenements of Glasgow: 'Second City'? . . . or 'Naples with bad weather'? This question was becoming insistent, as the Liberals swept to their greatest-ever victory in 1906, in the social planning movement of men like Professor Patrick Geddes.

17. Finest Hour

1914-18

IN 1904 the First Lord of the Admiralty, Lord Cawdor, commissioned a huge new turbine-powered, ten-heavy-gun battleship, HMS *Dreadnought*. At one step this made the 100-odd capital ships of the Royal Navy obsolete and triggered an expensive naval race with Germany. Speed, armour and guns escalated, though overhead and undersea new, far more deadly, weapons waited. Ten years later, the guns started firing.

Britain was dragged into World War One by treaty obligations to protect Belgium, but the conflict came after some years of intense political upheaval in practically every European state – the 1905 revolution in Russia, the Dreyfus Case in France, and labour conflicts overall – and secret compacts. John Buchan played a major role in propaganda, Sir William Weir in munitions production, while Sir Douglas Haig became Commander in Chief.

War propaganda was an early success which owed

A lady from hell . . . A poison dwarf . . .
See him, Kamerad, and run . . .

to the Scots involvement in mass literacy, ranging from Buchan's *Thirty-Nine Steps* and Ian Hay's *The First Hundred Thousand* to the apparently powerful documentation of German atrocities in Belgium in the Bryce Committee's report of 1915.

In May 1915 Lloyd George and his business allies, 'men of push and go', took on the business of outgunning Krupp, RheinStahl and Skoda, and won. The Germans don't seem to have believed that UK munitions production was possible on the scale achieved. Lloyd George's War Cabinet followed from this at the end of 1916 and two of its five members were Scots. The margin of their fight was narrow.

Austria and Turkey depended on the 'warfare state' of Germany. Of the allies, the Russian steamroller never got properly moving: a primitive road and rail system, aristocratic incompetence and corruption saw to that. The Germans set out to wear the French away at the fortress of Verdun, inspiring the first great British push to relieve them, at the Somme in June–November 1916. A bloodbath, it still showed the power the UK had in reserve.

In early 1917 Tsarist Russia collapsed, and desperate measures were taken to keep the unstable Russian republic in the war. In vain: French and

In Athens in 1918 British Intelligence was Major
Compton Mackenzie; his assistant was Lieutenant
Saunders Lewis. Within a decade they would found,

British offensives ended in terrible slaughter, and
there was menace at sea – not from the German fleet,
after the drawn battle of Jutland in May 1916 – but
from near-lethal, 'unrestricted U-boat warfare'. Clyde
shipyards had to replace the losses, though in April
1917 this brought the USA into the war, just as the
Bolsheviks took Russia out. For the period until US
troops arrived Britain stood against Germany with,
as Haig put it, 'our backs to the wall'.

The army that pressed eastwards from Cambrai
in mid-1918 was far different from the tiny force that
had landed in Belgium in 1914. Thousands of brand-
new weapons had been manufactured for it – planes,
trucks, tanks, machine-guns, bombs, and millions
of tons of high-explosive shells. 'Dilution' of the
labour-force enabled this. 30,000 out of 57,000
Clydeside munitions workers were women by 1918,
when those over 30 were rewarded with the vote.
But this pressure changed and distorted the
machinery and methods of the Clyde, making any
return to peacetime trade difficult. . .

. . . for those who stayed. The left journalist Lord
Ritchie-Calder said of the troops who left his home
town of Forfar: 'They marched to the station, and
they never came back.'

---

respectively, the National Party of Scotland (1928)
and Plaid Cymru, the Party of Wales (1925).
Unknown to them Christopher Grieve was working
as a medical orderly in Thessalonika.

'Were they killed?'

'No. they just didn't come back.'

There was also another secretive war to do with
promoting nations against empires, where Scotland's
cosmopolitanism played its part, whether through
R.W. Seton-Watson among the south Slavs, Arthur
Balfour and the Jews, the half-Scots T.E. Lawrence
and the Arabs. Lord Bryce tried to help the
Armenians, and authored the 'covenant' idea behind
the League of Nations. Why not – with Ireland's 1916
rebellion in mind – come closer to home?

Within the two-party system, the war caused an
earthquake. In 1906 the Liberals had a near-
monopoly of Scots MPs. By 1922 they had been
overtaken by Labour, swollen by the 'Red Clyde' –
growing trade unionism – and the wider franchise
granted in 1918. After 1939 the party of Gladstone
all but disappeared for twenty years.

PART III
CHOOSING A FUTURE

18. Depression and Renaissance

1920-1955

UNEMPLOYMENT and emigration branded Scotland during the 1920s: 'that depressed region'. After making good wartime losses, postwar exhaustion kept joblessness around 14%, worsening to 22% in the early 1930s. Roughly 10% of the population left the country for England and – until the catastrophic Wall Street slump of 1929 – overseas.

The heavy industries contracted or were 'rationalised' but generally survived. It was the smaller, locally owned firms making general machinery and consumer goods that went to the wall, carrying much of the country's enterprise culture with them. Many of the radical promises of the Lloyd George government were forgotten, though electrification expanded with the creation of the national grid, the telephone system grew, and for many families the cinema, particular after the talkies in 1929, replaced the Kirk.

Quite different, and so small-scale in its units of organisation as to come in 'under the radar' was the 'Scottish renaissance' which began in the middle of the 1920s under a remarkable figure: Christopher Grieve, 'Hugh MacDiarmid'. MacDiarmid was a fine lyric poet and critic but possessed of a mission to drag the country on to its feet as a European nation. He was hopeless at party politics but as dramatic as Thomas Carlyle – 'a bolt of lightning in a china shop' – as a mobiliser and cultural liberator. Other writers clustered round him: Eric Linklater, Neil Gunn, Lewis Grassic Gibbon, Sorley MacLean. Culturally, this investment would pay off in five decades, even if politically the prospects for nationalism looked near-hopeless.

> O Scotland is
> The barren fig.
> Up, carles, up
> An' roond it jig.

> Old Moses took
> A dry stick and
> Instantly it
> Floo'red in his hand.

Pu' Scotland up,
An' wha can say
It winna bud
An blossom tae!

A miracle's
Oor only chance
Up, carles, up
And let us dance!

Was the rise of the Labour party under its Scots leader, Ramsay Macdonald, minority Prime Minister at Westminster in 1924 and 1929, any compensation? A trade union and councillor oligarchy squeezed out the ethical socialists of the Independent Labour Party (ILP), and the National Party of Scotland was largely a 1928 secession from the ILP. Both made little progress, in comparison with the disproportionately Scots-led Communists in the trade unions.

Yet equally fruitless was the General Strike of May 1926, when railwaymen and dockers came out across Scotland to support the miners, whose wages were to be cut. It was well-behaved and unsuccessful, and this diverted the unions from direct action to building up Labour's control of local government. They won Glasgow, Aberdeen and Dundee by 1935, and stayed put until the new century. Socialism meant the take-over of housing through state subsidy and local authority ownership, a policy begun by the ablest of the Clydesiders, John Wheatley, during the brief Labour government of 1924.

A stronger Labour minority regime took office under MacDonald in 1929, only to be hit when the Crash ended the USA's post-war boom. The Cabinet struggled with mounting unemployment, but refused to back expenditure cuts. MacDonald with King George V's support formed a National Government largely of Conservatives, which slaughtered his old party at the 1931 election. He then talked vaguely about devolution.

The leaders of business showed hostile, but one of them, the Clydeside magnate Sir James Lithgow, helped create such economic institutions as the Scottish National Development Council, incorporated into interventionist government by a remarkable Tory, Walter Elliot. In fact, with the relaunch of the Scottish National Party (1933) in the background, progressive patriotism had a good decade, unlike elsewhere in Europe where it was seen off by drums and marching men. Rearmament took the edge off the depression after 1935, and Secretary Elliot managed a brief fest of Art Deco with the commissioning of the 'Queen Mary', the 1938 Glasgow Empire Exhibition and St Andrews House.

Scotland's hour, however, came again with war. As the hinge of Europe and the Atlantic, it was a strategic key. In 1940 it became a base for Norwegian and Polish loyalists, driven into exile by the German *blitzkrieg*. From 1941 it hosted the Americans, first with lend-lease aid, then with planes and troops; Prestwick became Europe's busiest airport. After Russia joined the allies, its naval bases and sea lochs were the junctions where convoys were marshalled for the eastern front.

Prime Minister Winston Churchill made an inspired choice in Tom Johnston, his foe as a journalist on the Red Clyde, as Secretary of State. Johnston built up Scotland's transit and supply role, while planning great hydro-electric schemes for the Highlands, carried out between 1945-62. He gave bipartisan social reform, in the Beveridge Report of 1942, a strong Scottish accent. But on the whole the experience of the war, and the heroic leading role of London, 'Churchill's city', bolstered a British ethos which took a generation to fade.

Electrical power generated in Scotland rose from 1900 Megawatt hours (MWh) in 1939 to 3017 in 1961, 10,378 in 1978 and 48,217 in 2007. The watt was named after James Watt. It wasn't being used in manufacturing, 66% of Gross Domestic Product in 1935, 44% in 1976, and 16% in 2009.

Clement Attlee and Labour, elected rather surprisingly in 1945 (though its success in Scotland was less sweeping) added to this with the Welfare State, the National Health Service and the nationalisation of the service industries: coal, electricity and gas, steel, docks, aviation, buses, railways. The Scots were generally grateful, but a bit breathtaken by the centralisation involved, and there was a large-scale though short-lived nationalist reaction, the Covenant movement, directed by John MacCormick, earlier first Secretary of the SNP. On the rim of all this, on the Isle of Jura, George Orwell wrote a book about how freedom depended on language and history: *1984*. Around him, Gaelic was dying out.

Labour decreed a Festival of Britain for 1951, held in London. Churchill, back with his Tories in that year, had his return match with the Coronation of Elizabeth II in 1953. Balmoral was reborn for the TV age, but the magic didn't last.

Scotland's summers get wetter and wetter – fact.
So, aff tae Tenerife!

19. Administrative Devolution

1945-74

THE AFTERMATH of World War Two was, on the surface, far different from the disaster of the 1920s. Because German and Japanese shipyards and engineering works were heaps of rubble, industrial Scotland had a second boom. But little investment was going into the traditional industries, and although there were some attempts at consumer goods (in 1950 Dundee made more clocks than Switzerland) small houses and low incomes still inhibited these. Scotland was stuck back in its own 1900s, not even getting to the English 1930s.

For the Empire, though still extensive, was proving impossible to hold. The fall of Singapore in 1942 had been its death sentence; this was carried out when Britain and France attacked the Suez Canal in 1956 to capture the pivotal imperial link. They were repulsed, not just by Colonel Nasser's Egyptian nationalists but by John Foster Dulles at the US State Department.

While Suez was closed, the size of tankers soared, from 40,000 to over 250,000 tons, far too big to be built on the Clyde. Shrewd bosses took the hint and invested in greenfield sites in South Korea. Railways declined – temporarily – but enough to kill off the steam-age Glasgow locomotive industry. The Scottish coalfield, fading away for years in its main centre of Lanarkshire, faced first hydro-electricity, then nuclear power. A similar but slower nemesis overtook textiles, cookers, furniture, porcelain, linoleum, carpets.

Labour benefited from the political backlash, and after Harold Wilson's government, 1964-70 and its planning solutions came unstuck (its one real success, the Open University, was Scots in inspiration) the reviving SNP stood ready. But Scots commerce found it difficult to compete. 'Would you rather shop at Marks and Sparks or the Co-op?' was the key question, and the old 'store' with its 'divvy', lack of credit, and fusty fashions lost out. The same went for small holiday resorts with dodgy weather when charter flights to the Mediterranean came in. By the 1970s the Scottish high street looked like

Only 2% of Scots commuters use Fleming and Dunlop's energy-efficient safety bike. They love their cars and spend over £12 billion a year on them, yet attempts at mass-manufacture, from the Argyll to the Hillman Imp, have all ended in failure.

anywhere else in the UK, but its people's politics were different. In 1955 the Tories with 50% support, had been top party; after 1959 Scotland was their weakest link.

Railways were torn up and mines closed, but an attempt in 1971 by the incoming Heath government to close most Clyde shipyards was met by a 'work-in' at the John Brown shipyard led by the remarkable duo of Jimmy Reid and Jimmy Airlie. Shrewd as well as brave, this saved equipment and skills to tackle the oil opportunity. Scots didn't much fancy entry to what became the European Union in 1975, though they voted for it. Later, Europe became popular, because someone down south didn't like it at all. My enemy's enemy is my friend!

'Swing, handbag, swing!'
North Sea oil bankrolls Margaret Thatcher

20. Black Oil, Iron Lady

1979-1997

OIL WAS FOUND in 1969 in the Montrose field 100 miles off Aberdeen. Discoveries multiplied and in 1978 the 'black stuff' was being pumped ashore, just as output rose to a first peak in 1986. A second came in 1999. At its highest it made up 4% of UK Gross National Product (GNP). The Norwegians had nationalised production in 1971 with Statoil, and by 2007 their GNP per capita was more than $90,000. Scotland's was about half that, which would not have surprised the SNP, who had made a new politics out of the new resource, and in 1974 looked like becoming top party.

Yet they were outwitted by the Labour Party, which promised devolution *and* an oil fund but in fact shrewdly divided the Scots. A devolution bill was laboriously put through Westminster by James Callaghan and John Smith, but failed at a referendum in 1979.

Three months later Mrs Thatcher took power, and

TV's principle goes back to Clerk Maxwell's
experiments in 1860s. First demonstrated by John
Logie Baird in 1925, two years after John Reith's
BBC, TV reached Scotland in 1952, 'saturating'

lasted until 1990. In a sort of black farce, the oil-propelled petropound shot up to nearly $40 a barrel, driven further by the first Iran-Iraq Gulf War and monetarism's high interest rates. This priced UK exports out of world markets, and chopped 20% of Scottish manufacturing.

In Scotland Thatcher was hated, and not just by her opponents. 'That bloody woman' or 'TBW' as Scots Tories referred to her, destroyed her own party. From 26 MPs out of 73 in 1979 they fell to 22 in 1983 and to 10 in 1987. In fact her Scottish Secretary George Younger cleverly manoeuvred to keep many Scots interest groups happy, for instance by fighting to keep the Royal Bank Scots and for the Scottish steel industry, while both Labour and the SNP convulsed themselves with internal strife.

But subsidies to housing were cut, much of the stock sold off to 'upwardly-mobile' tenants, and the numbers living in poverty rose from 10% to 25% of the population. Drug use soared in areas traumatised by factory closures, and inept decision-making led to an increase of HIV infection. Irvine Welsh and Danny Boyle marketed this as Scottish urban gothic in *Trainspotting*, book and 1996 film. If you were a man in the most-depressed ward in Glasgow, Calton,

Scots homes by 1970. Alexander Graham Bell's
telephone came in UK-wide in the 1880s, but
there was only one phone per 10 Scots in 1963;
'saturation' came after 1990.

you would on average die before age 60.

The bright spots in the economy were two. The first would prove transient: 'Silicon Glen', a swathe of hi-tech manufacturing, by the late 1980s extended from Ayr to Aberdeen. It grew fast but was concentrated on 'screwdriver' manufacturing of hardware – mobile phones, computers, printers – which could easily be transferred elsewhere if works had to be re-equipped or the labour force grew stroppy.

The Irish concentrated on pharmaceuticals and software, and prospered: about two-thirds as wealthy as the Scots in the 1970s, by 2000 they had gone ahead. By then, little of Silicon Glen remained but the shiny shells of empty factories. In financial services Edinburgh built on its rescued Royal Bank and made huge sums out of Thatcher's and John Major's privatisations and the mortgage boom after the council house sell-off. Banking expertise helped Scottish entrepreneurs such as Brian Souter of Stagecoach and Moir Lochhead of First to make fortunes out of bus and rail privatisation.

The Scots voters got their act together and voted tactically to put Conservatives out, successfully in the 1987 election. Then Labour and the Liberals backed a Constitutional Convention to plan an agreed scheme of self-government. It first met in 1989 and was steered by its Convenor, the Rev Canon Kenyon Wright, into producing a report which contained devolution, which most Labourites wanted, and proportional representation for the new parliament, an old LibDem cause. The era of single-party dominance would go into eclipse.

The churches whom Canon Wright represented were already there. They had still record numbers of adherents in the 1960s, but thereafter declined rapidly. The Protestants were first to tumble, but were soon followed by the Catholics. Neither church had taken women seriously, although they had traditionally kept congregations together. Now they had more interesting things to do – education, careers – and left in droves.

22. Strands of
Molten Cheese
1997-2010

IN MAY 1997 the last Scots Tory MPs were wiped out. IN SEPTEMBER 1997 the Scots had voted for devolution by 74% to 26%. Labour politicians believed that this concession would 'kill nationalism stone dead', yet a minority SNP government was elected less than ten years later and even enjoyed popularity. Independence sentiment reached 40%, close behind support for devolution. Why?

The two Lib-Lab coalitions 1999-2003 (under Donald Dewar, Henry McLeish and Jack McConnell) and 2003-2007 (under McConnell) had not tackled the country's underlying problems: high levels of 'real' unemployment and consequent poverty, the expansion of 'jobs for the boys' micro-management, the stagnation of the small and medium enterprise (SME) sector. There was much anger at Labour's foreign policy – the war in Iraq, the new Trident nuclear weapons – and at oil revenues being used to fund an artificial UK prosperity, based on the real estate/retailing motor, while long-term investment in renewable energy and essential infrastructure, sustainable housing and public transport, was neglected.

In the 2007 election the swing to the SNP (47 seats) was considerable, but largely at the expense of the Scottish Socialists and the Greens, who fell from 13 to two MSPs. Labour still held 46 seats, but it lost heavily also in May 2007 with the introduction of PR to local government, retaining majority control of only two authorities, Glasgow and North Lanarkshire. The Liberals were demoralised and the Conservatives made no progress.

SNP leader Alex Salmond ran a powerful propaganda campaign, backed by prominent businessmen, notably Sir George Mathewson of the Royal Bank and Brian Souter of Stagecoach, while still offering a social-democrat agenda. His coup was to go for a minority government, calculating that by seizing the machinery of power, he could consolidate the SNP advantage.

Labour Prime Minister Tony Blair and later Gordon Brown obliged by sulking in London (communications with Whitehall were minimal, though good with the devolved governments in Belfast and Cardiff) while their party lost morale in Scotland.

Coalitions usually compromise on spending policies – simplifying 'who cut what' problems – but a minority government hadn't this excuse. Moreover Whitehall's Consolidated Spending Review was severe. The SNP's actions were populist – freezing local taxes, granting rates rebates to small businesses, ending tolls on road bridges. This was paid for by reducing the budgets of Scottish Enterprise, widely regarded as inefficient, and devolving much administration to local authorities in an 'historic concordat'. Although there was controversy over details, the government's openness was welcomed.

Even in summer 2007, however, strange writing was on the wall: SIVs, CDOs, CDOs-squared, CDSs. Chancellor Brown's enthusiasm for the 'lighter-than-air' world of financial services led London to become open house for speculators, and this infected hitherto douce Edinburgh and its two major banks – the Royal Bank and Halifax Bank of Scotland. UK investment in 'sub-prime securities' (basically, loaning money to Homer Simpson) seemed to rival the hysteria of

On 8 August 2010 David Cameron announced that welfare and tax credit fraud and error (by the unemployed/unfit) cost the taxpayer £5.2bn a year. 'That's the cost of more than 200 secondary schools or over 150,000 nurses.' In June 2006 leaked

John Law's exploits in the 1720s and in the autumn of 2008 it ran out of road. Other European countries had used their banks to manoeuvre internationally for independence, Salmond likewise. But after Christmas 2008 there was no Scots banking system left.

310 years on, 'Scotland's pinstripe Darien' brought the country to earth with a terrible bump. The RBS and HBOS were dragged south and much of the Edinburgh financial centre followed them. Credit was tightened for small firms, the last locally-owned manufacturers came under threat. In 2007 the journalist Andrew Marr had written of the Union resembling a pizza with a slice being slowly removed until all that held it together were 'strands of molten cheese'. Yet in the May 2010 Westminster election, which saw Gordon Brown on the ropes yet no great enthusiasm outside the English south for the Conservative David Cameron, *nothing in Scotland changed*. Seat by seat, the result was the same as 2005.

Things throve that Holyrood didn't want to thrive: the bonuses of a banking system saved by the

> Treasury papers revealed that the government
> estimated an annual loss of between £97 billion and
> £157 billion to tax theft (by the wealthy). This
> represented 8% to 12% of UK GDP, or the total
> value of Scotland's output. (BBC, 9th August, 2010;
> Adam Taylor, *Guardian*, 10th January 2007).

taxpayer but driven by a greed and complicity in
'moral hazard' which had run out of control. Would
Cameron's cuts hit the gentry in their big houses and
4x4s who were in but not of the countryside? Dream
on . . .

Other big houses and big cars contained drug
barons whose trade continued to colonised Scots
housing estates, its recycled cash propelling a 'rest
and recreation economy' which was probably bigger
than SME manufacturing. Supermarkets siphoned
prosperity out of small towns, and into the vacuum
came tanning and nail and tattoo parlours, take-
aways, night clubs, whose ownership was obscure.

Alcohol, whose real price had fallen by half over
this period, became an alternative addiction, or
browsing on cheap food from supermarkets or take-
aways. By 2010 about two-thirds of Scots 'living
unhealthily', and a national taste for 'sportswear' –
among drivers or telly-addicts – had the Scots
catching up on the Americans in the Sumo stakes.
And was 'Jockney' enticing? A style not a dialect
(fewer wrote with accuracy in a verbal, not a literate,
age), too often using the f-word as noun, verb,

adjective, adverb, conjunction, preposition, exclamation.

This was superficial, and only part of the story. Crime was falling and (to the degree this could be measured) people were living happier and more fulfilled lives, looking after the old, the chronically ill and the handicapped, contributing generously to charities, conserving the environment. The problem remained one of inequality, lack of hope, and social isolation: the Glasgow Calton situation. For those in the suburbs, among the middle class, missions and settlements and political work gave way to foreign holidays and second homes. This was in a society where people were anyway more mobile, and different life-stages might involve different environments, but a new Godly – or secular – Commonwealth had yet to arrive.

In 2010 ideas about ways forward seemed divergent, but not straightforward. Towards independence? Certainly Scotland was less and less inhibited by British institutions, many factories and utilities being foreign-owned. Buying into the Great Power game meant a huge cost in arms. Or did the great chance lie in the seas which had surged round the place since the last ice age, the swells that rolled in from the Atlantic, the currents of the Minches and the Pentland Firth? These could provide over 20% of the energy needs of a Europe facing peak oil at around $200 a barrel. In 2010 it was already over $80. The Scots could be masters of this if they assessed priorities and invested wisely. They had no other chance.

23. 'Stands Scotland where it did?'

. . . asks MacDuff in *Macbeth*, and gets a pile of articulate grievances dropped on him. Not easy to generalise about, identity in Scotland has always operated at several levels, between family and empire. A nation of five ethnies, yet unified by the eleventh century, it came in with a top-heavy, privileged politico-religious class, whose talents were exportable – to Scandinavia and France as well as (up to 1300) England. Anglo-Scottish confrontation up to 1560 was exceptional rather than the norm. It couldn't really function after the latter powered towards sea-dominance. This both required and fostered the integrity of the islands, but didn't chance a crushing English hegemony.

The consequence was that links and arguments were open – both between the Scottish 'estates' and between the two countries – even when contradictions were seen from outside. Parliament (and its nobles) was always rivalled by the Kirk, especially after 1707, and within the elite by the Advocates, the Universities, the Burghs. Scots traded with the Veere staple regardless of England's wars. The balance changed after the 1745 rebellion: the military society of the Highlands adopted political goals, also shifting from Europe to the empire.

So Thomas Carlyle's gospel of work, seemingly non-national, could imply a dismissal of English deference as servility. The 'raucle tung' of the Doric had its own percussive discourse, from Burns to Buchan and MacDiarmid. There were parallels in German regionalism, as well as in the hybrid societies within the British Empire where received pronunciation was a disadvantage. UK cultural unity had proved as transitory as nationality had been, and without it prospects for federalism weren't good.

The present confrontation – with a Conservatism lacking a Scottish mandate – shifts back to the 1630s and the Three Kingdoms situation, with Westminster's using reserved subjects as today's 'Lords of the Articles'. But Westminster's ambitions haven't checked the City or restored its own international clout, just as Ireland couldn't rescue its economic miracle from its plutocrats.

What lies ahead? The Anglo-Scottish union was never federal, and after 1999 the two countries, though held together by UK Labour government, absent-mindedly but effectively divorced. Development possibilities became quite different, as military and financial power finally ran out.

A confederal covenant within the islands would be valuable, and may in embryo lie with the British-Irish Secretariat, now based in Edinburgh. But the literal mechanism for this is renewable power deployed against peak oil. Can this co-exist with Trident and giant aircraft carriers? Or must the last enchantments of imperialism be ploughed under?

* * *

Appendices

(1) HISTORY TO VISIT

Not a guide, but a follow-up to history in print or on film. The concentration is on 'Central Scotland': because most key events happened in places reachable in a day trip from Edinburgh/ Glasgow/ Dundee. For 'Further afield' places, which need at least an overnight stop, scenery and recreation outweigh history.

Key websites (www.+):
1. travel: travelinescotland.com; scotrail.co.uk; stagecoachbus.com; firstgroup.com/ukbus/
2. places: visitscotland.com; nts.org.uk; historic-scotland.gov.uk; nms.ac.uk; nationalgalleries.org; scran.ac.uk

CENTRAL SCOTLAND
Ayr: Robert Burns's Country: his birthplace in Alloway, the ruined kirk and bridge out of 'Tam o' Shanter'. Robert Adam's nearby Culzean Castle shows the grand style of the lairds who patronised and exploited him.

Bute: Sail from Wemyss Bay (John Miller's splendid railway pier) to Rothesay, the Blackpool of Glasgow, and the extraordinary Florentine-gothic Mount Stuart mansion, built by the Marquess of Bute in 1880.

Clyde: The P.S. 'Waverley' (1947: last seagoing paddler in the world) visits the lochs and islands of the Clyde each summer. Arran, almost a miniature Scotland, Lochs Long and Fyne with fine mountains, Inveraray Castle, from which the Campbells ruled Scotland. The Trident submarines in Loch Long have enough nukes to blow us all to blazes.

Dundee: 'Juteopolis', the most imperial of Scots cities, made its cash from Calcutta hemp, pressed with whale oil. See the Verdant Factory and on the Tay the Antarctic research ship 'Discovery', based on whaling design. Famous for D.C. Thomson, keepers of Desperate Dan and Dennis the Menace. Across the Tay St Andrews, Scotland's first University (1411) and centre of Reformation and Mecca of Golf.

Edinburgh: with municipal (extinct) volcanoes, Arthur's Seat and Castlehill, medieval Old Town and classical New Town, grand museums and galleries, St Giles Kirk and Miralles' remarkable Parliament (2004). On outskirts Roslin, its ornate Chapel (1446) made legendary by Dan Brown, not to speak of Dolly the cloned sheep.

Falkirk and Linlithgow: Linlithgow Palace and Kirk show the Stewarts doing the grand style. Falkirk marked the start of smelting by coal with its Carron Ironworks, 1766. The Forth and Clyde Canal has the Falkirk Wheel (2000) connecting it to the Union Canal. At nearby Bo'ness see the Forth road and rail bridges and Scottish Railway Museum with working branch line. Blackness Castle was Elsinore in Mel Gibson's *Hamlet*; better than his *Braveheart*.

Fife: 'a beggar's mantle fringed with gold', reached by amazing bridges. Dunfermline famous as first royal capital, and birthplace of Andrew Carnegie; royal hunting palace at Falkland; Kirkcaldy for linoleum and Adam Smith; Anstruther for Scottish Fisheries Museum.

Glasgow: the magnificent St Mungo's Cathedral, (12th century) and Charles Rennie Mackintosh's 1910 Art College are European wonders. See also the Burrell Collection, Kelvingrove Art Galleries and Zahya Hadid's Riverside Museum of Transport.

Loch Lomond and the Trossachs: Made famous by Sir Walter Scott's 'The Lady of the Lake' and a halfday introduction to the Highlands by bus, boat and on Loch Katrine, vintage steamer called – you've guessed! – 'Sir Walter Scott'.

Melrose and Abbotsford: The Border Abbeys matured from being isolated hermitages to wool and wealth, Melrose being the most opulent. It marked the start of Scott's historical 'Waverley Novel' sequence (1814-27) whose income built his Abbotsford mansion (1812), almost a purpose-built literary factory.

New Lanark: Scotland's finest monument from the first industrial revolution, the four water-powered cotton mills built by David Dale in 1785, and used by Robert Owen for social experiment. Nearby Biggar is a small Victorian town with several museums.

Paisley: famous for cotton-reels and fabulous shawls. **Port Glasgow** (1683) marked the beginning of the Clyde's mercantile growth. **Greenock** boomed first with sugar, then with ships, then with IBM Europe. Where now?

Perth: next to old coronation site of Scone. Gateway to Highlands with a huge station. North-east of Aviemore the whisky distilleries of the Spey valley. The Scots Reformation began in St. John's Kirk, but fine Edwardian City Hall under threat.

Stirling and Bannockburn: A key river-crossing to the north, commanded by an acropolis. At its bridge, Wallace's coup of 1297 destroyed the English army. In 1314, Bruce's victory confirmed Scots independence on Bannockburn field. Not far off the tiny 17th century trading port of Culross.

FURTHER AFIELD:

Aberdeen: City of Grey Granite, most astonishing at medieval St Machar's and Victorian Marischal College; oil has made it a bustling port (see the huge model production platform in Maritime Museum on the Quay); Queen Victoria's Balmoral, in castle country, is 60 miles west.

Inverness: Grand and pious Victorian city, blighted by supermarkets, but see Culloden Battlefield and Fort George and try to see Nessie (no-one has: making a non-thing as tourist attraction gets close to genius!) but gentle scenery and pleasant excursion boats on Telford's Caledonian Canal to Fort William. West and north lie the lands 'cleared' for sheep and deer.

Orkney and Shetland: Norse Scotland contains unequalled monuments from the Stone Age (Skara Brae, Maes Howe, Mousa Broch), the Viking age (Brough of Birsay) and the medieval grandeur of Kirkwall Cathedral and Earl's Palace. The culture of both archipelagos has thrived from being remote, and benefited from the oil boom.

West Highland Railway: Links Glasgow with the seaports of Oban and Mallaig, where ferries run to Mull and Columba's Iona and to Skye. From Kyle another spectacular line runs to Inverness and to the far north at Thurso and Wick. Bus to Ullapool for ferry to the Gaelic-speaking, tweed-weaving Outer Hebrides.

(2) THE SCOTTISH YEAR
(see F Marian MacNeill, *The Silver Bough*, 1956).
These fests aren't just important in themselves;
they show when places get booked out!

31 Dec-1 Jan	Hogmanay (Yule)
January Fest	Celtic Connections, Glasgow
25 January	Burns Night
last Tues in Jan	Up Helly AA!, Fire Festival, Lerwick
17 March	St Patrick's Day
30 April	Beltane Fest in Edinburgh
1 May	May Day/Labour Movement Marches
May	Church of Scotland General Assembly. Edinburgh Seven-a-Side Rugby Competitions, Borders
end of May	Orkney Festival
June	Border Common Ridings (Hawick, Lauder, Selkirk. Langholm, Jedburgh)
20-26 June	Beltane Fest in Peebles)

July/August	Holyrood Parliament in Recess. Kinross: 'T(ennents) in the Park': Kinross's Glastonbury; Edinburgh/Glasgow Trades/Fair holidays
12 July	Protestant 'marching season', colourful, until you make out the lyrics
12 August	'Glorious Twelfth': grouse-shooting season opens
August	Edinburgh Festival and Fringe (Europe's biggest culture bash) 'Cowal Fortnight' regatta, Clyde; Festival of Politics. Holyrood Highland Games season
September	Mod (Gaelic literary fest) in Highland towns
29 October	Halloween: 'ghaists and bogles' not 'trick or treat'
11 November	Armistice Day: wreath-laying ceremonies on Sunday
30 November	St Andrew's Day
25 December	Christmas (still a working day in the 1960s)

(3) TWENTY BOOKS ABOUT SCOTLAND

Sources:
Rosemary Goring, *Scotland: the Autobiography*,
     London: Penguin, 2008.
Louise Yeomans, *Reportage Scotland*,
     Edinburgh: Luath, 2000.

General and Political History
Michael Fry, *Patronage and Principle: A Political
     History of Modern Scotland*, Aberdeen
     University Press, 1987.
Michael Fry, *The Scottish Empire*, Edinburgh:
     Birlinn, 2001.
Richard Finlay, *Modern Scotland*, London:
     Profile, 2004.
RAB Houston and Bill Knox, eds., *The New
     Penguin History of Scotland*, London:
     Penguin, 2001.
Christopher Harvie, *A Floating Commonwealth*,
     Oxford, 2008.
James Mitchell, *Strategies for Self-Government*,
     Edinburgh: Polygon, 1996.
Kenneth O Morgan, ed., *The Oxford History of
     Britain*, Oxford UP, 1983.

Social History:
Bechhofer, McCrone and Paterson, *Living in
     Scotland*, Edinburgh University Press, 2004.
Tom Devine, *The Scottish Nation*, London:
     Penguin 1999.
Bill Knox, *Industrial Nation*, Edinburgh
     University Press, 1999.

John Ransom, *Iron Road: the Railway in Scotland* , Edinburgh: Birlinn, 2006.

Christopher Smout, *A History of the Scottish People, 1560-1830*, Glasgow: Collins, 1969.

Christopher Smout, *A Century of the Scottish People, l830-l950*, Glasgow: Collins, l986.

Cultural and Art History:

Cairns Craig et al., eds., *The History of Scottish Literature*, 4 Vols., Aberdeen University Press, 1988-1990.

Robert Crawford, *Scotland's Books*, Penguin, 2008.

Billy Kay, *The Scottish World*, Edinburgh: Mainstream, 2006.

Duncan Macmillan, *Scottish Art, 1460-1990*, Edinburgh: Mainstream, 1990.

Sean Connery and Murray Grigor, *Being a Scot*, London: Weidenfeld, 2008.

Scotsman (daily newspaper): www.scotsman.com

Herald (daily newspaper) and *Sunday Herald*: www.theherald.co.uk

Scottish Affairs www.scottish.affairs.org

Scottish Review of Books www.scottishreviewofbooks.org

Scottish Parliament: www.scottishparliament.uk

Political facts and polls: www.alba.org.uk

see also www.conservativeparty.org.uk

www.labour org.uk, www.snp.org.uk

Index